Going for Growth

what works at
local church level

CHURCH HOUSE
PUBLISHING

Bob Jackson

Church House Publishing
Church House
Great Smith Street
London SW1P 3NZ
Tel: 020 7898 1451
Fax: 020 7898 1449

ISBN-13 978-0-7151-4107-6
ISBN-10 0 7151-4107-4

Published 2006 by Church House Publishing

Typeset in Rotis Semi Sans by RefineCatch Ltd, Bungay, Suffolk

Printed in England by MPG Books Ltd, Bodmin, Cornwall

Contents

A guidebook for all
PCCs
Cell groups
House groups
Lent groups
Leadership groups
Individuals

who are concerned about the growth and future of the Church

Introduction

I love seeing human lives changed for the better through a church introducing individuals to Jesus Christ. I love seeing churches transform their communities and change society. I love seeing churches flourish and grow.

If you do too, then use this book to explore with others what can be done locally where you are. Its ideas and conclusion are based on factual research of the church scene in Britain today. This shows that, although it is true that the churches have been in numerical decline now for around a century, there are many signs of new hope and growth.

The latest data shows that the Church of England may now have stopped shrinking numerically. The 'usual Sunday attendance' of adults actually went up very slightly in 2004 for the first time in many years. Many individual churches and some groups and dioceses are growing strongly. The membership (electoral roll) of the Diocese of London has gone up by a half in the last fifteen years.

But do remember that churches fixated on growth rarely grow. Quantity normally flows naturally from quality and relevance. Growing churches have found God's way for them to offer high quality relevance to the people around them. As every church and every situation is unique, then God's way to grow will be different in every church – so please find in this book no standard techniques but rather stimulus, ideas, options and inspiration.

And what you will find is not rocket science. Most of the ways of growing that churches have found are straightforward and open to others. And ours is not the ultimate responsibility. Jesus is the same as ever – ready, willing and able to grow his church just so long as we provide him with some favourable conditions so he can breathe new life into it. In the Christian Church, expect dry bones to live, the moribund to spring to life and the God of resurrection to triumph again.

Bob Jackson
Easter Sunday 2006

How to use this book

This book is about how churches are growing and the lessons that can be learnt from their growth. You will find the evidence and arguments laid out in full in my book *The Road to Growth* (Church House Publishing 2005), and also in *Hope for the Church* (Church House Publishing 2002). As your group goes through the book, it would help if at least one of you has read *The Road to Growth* and you have a reference copy of the book with you.

You will find summaries, arranged in eight sections, of the factors associated with the numerical growth of churches.

- Growing the Church through **good practice**
- Growing the Church through **change**
- Growing the Church through **fresh expressions**
- Growing the Church through **diocesan policy and shared values**
- Growing the Church through **deploying the clergy**
- Growing the Church through **lay leadership and training**
- Growing the Church through **sound finances**
- Growing the Church through **spiritual renewal**

Your group will probably wish to study one section a week through an eight-week course, but you could spend a shorter time in discussion once all of you have read the book as a whole.

Putting the book into practice

1. Check out your own church against the different ways of growing listed here. What are we doing right and what is going wrong?

2. Work out the options that may in practice be available to you.

3. Discuss and pray through what might be God's growth priorities for your own church and formulate some sort of strategy, plan or initiative.

4. Be creative in the way you adopt and adapt the lessons learnt, bearing in mind your local situation.

5. Develop a new confidence, vision and determination that the growth of the church is possible and also an integral part of the mission to which God calls you.

If this book is all you have, then you will have to take most of the factual and numerical evidence lying behind these factors on trust – this evidence is laid out in full in the book *The Road to Growth*, which is why it is helpful to have a copy available.

Further resources

Anglican Church Planting Initiatives
acpi.org.uk/index.html

Back to Church Sunday
backtochurch.co.uk

Diocese of London
london.anglican.org/CapitalIdea

The Fresh Expressions web site
freshexpressions.org.uk

Leading Your Church into Growth Courses
Tim.Sledge@peterborough-diocese.org.uk

Sheffield Church Army Centre for Church Planting web site
churcharmy.org.uk/ChurchArmy/web/site/ChurchArmy/
TheSheffieldCentre/SheffieldCentreHome.asp

1

Growing the Church through good practice

(The Road to Growth Chapter 5)

This section comes from a variety of surveys finding links between features of church life and their numerical trends.

It is about good practices for the planting and growing of churches:

> *I planted, Apollos watered, but God gave the growth . . .*
> *neither the one who plants nor the one who waters is*
> *anything, but only God who gives the growth.*
>
> *1 Corinthians 3.6–7*

1. **Care for the clergy.** On average, churches grow best between around the fifth and twelfth years of the vicar or minister's time with them. It often takes a while for trust to grow and strategies to mature. Eventually, though, things may get stale, in a rut. It is clearly important that your vicar or minister stays fresh and enthusiastic.

   Have your clergy ever left too soon? How well do you care for your clergy? How might you give them time for personal renewal, so that they stay physically and spiritually fresh?

2. **Aim for a wide age spread.** Churches shrink older and grow younger. Numerical growth usually involves younger generations joining the church and contributing their energy and freshness to it.

   What is your church's age structure at the moment, and

what are you doing to make your church attractive to the younger half of the population?

3. **Use evangelism courses.** Courses such as Alpha and Emmaus are a good way of accompanying people on their journey into faith. But they are only really associated with church growth if they are part of a regular programme that includes ways of making new contacts and next-stage provision at the end of the course.

Do you offer courses regularly and how well integrated are they into your church's regular programme? What courses might be most suitable?

4. **Provide for teenagers.** This is often a key element in growth. Without it the children know they are expected to leave when they are twelve. Good teenage ministry leads to membership of young adults and also of parents of teenagers. Churches that invest in youth ministry and youth worship attract young people. Those with professional youth ministers tend to do best of all.

What is the quality of your provision? Do you have a generous budget for it? If not, how can you provide a good budget?

5. **Use appropriate service times.** Churches are losing people at early communions and Sunday evenings, and gaining them later on Sunday mornings and at weekday worship events. Teatime on Saturday or Sunday is becoming a good time for services involving children. Young people and young adults without children are the only natural Sunday evening groupings.

Are your service times determined by historical accident or are they best fitted to the twenty-first century world? Is there a case for trying different timings?

6. **Use appropriate service styles.** Churches that vary the style at the same service time tend to create internal tension and some people stay away on certain Sundays. In today's variegated society (e.g. in music tastes) churches that stick to

one culture for all their services tend to attract only one narrow segment of the population. But Anglicans are supposed to be here for everyone! Growing churches tend to target specific services at specific people-groups – such as a 9.30 a.m. communion for traditional Anglicans, an 11 a.m. Family Service, a 4 p.m. minority-language service and a 7 p.m. youth and young adult event. Unity comes from shared vision and purpose. Small or country churches that only have one service a week can still offer variety by coordinating what they do with each other. It is important that there is a weekly service in each place – it is very hard to grow a fortnightly or monthly congregation either spiritually or numerically.

Is your service pattern the result of a clearly thought out mission strategy for today or is it just the result of half-remembered changes from long ago? What would be an ideal pattern for your church?

The 10.30 a.m. service at St Mark's was an uneasy compromise between those who preferred tradition and those who liked informality, between the choir and the music group, between 'the straights' and 'the hallelujahs'. The 8 a.m. Holy Communion congregation was small and dwindling. This was closed and a new service started at 9.15 a.m. – straight, no-compromise traditional communion with hymns. The 10.30 service became unashamedly informal and contemporary. Peace broke out between the two main factions and numbers began to grow.

2

Growing the Church through change

(The Road to Growth Chapter 6)

This section comes from surveys of several hundred churches that were asked to list the changes they had made to their church life in recent years and also to give their numbers trend. In was crystal clear that churches that had not made changes were shrinking and churches that had made at least one of the listed changes were growing.

It is about a mature attitude to change in the Church:

> *Forgetting what lies behind and straining forward to what lies ahead, I press on towards the goal . . . Let those of us then who are mature be of the same mind.*
> *Philippians 3.13,14,15*

1. **Plant new congregations.** This is how the church has grown throughout the world for 2,000 years. It is how the Church of England grew in Victorian times, and it is the most important way in which churches are growing today. Many individual congregations reach a natural ceiling size long before the church building is full. It is important to have a missionary mindset so that we ask 'What people-groups are we trying to reach and what type of new event would help us do that?' There is a huge variety of possibilities for trying something new these days – the important thing is to try!

   When was the last time your church started a new congregation or worship opportunity? What should be your first priority?

2. **Make worship more relaxed.** Stiff services where the tension level rises when something goes wrong, the congregation never smiles at the preacher's jokes, and people habitually disapprove of innovation are conspicuously unattractive in today's culture. One survey found that the only universal feature of all growing churches throughout the world was the presence of joy and laughter in the congregation.

   How relaxed are newcomers on their first visit to your church? How can people feel at home and enjoy themselves in your services while still staying in touch with the holiness of God?

3. **Improve the music.** The style and quality of music are more important to people than ever. Many young people will join in church music only if they think they would look cool singing it in front of their friends. Cathedrals discovered long ago that investment in quality music pays off in congregation size.

   How good is your music and is its style appropriate? What steps can you take to make the music into something that attracts people to worship God in your church?

4. **Provide for children.** The number of children and young people in our churches has not gone down because they have become less spiritually minded – in fact they are more spiritually open and aware probably than any previous generation. The harvest is plentiful but the numbers have gone down because the labourers are few and the methods have not developed fast enough in a changing world. Churches establishing new groups, starting an 'all-age' service, or appointing a paid children or families or youth minister have turned their numbers round.

   When did you last review the nature and standard of your own provision? Can you offer your children something more, or better?

5. **Integrate newcomers.** Most people will properly join a church only if they make some friends and become part of its

community. The smile of the sidesperson, even being a friendly church, is not enough. If people make two or three friends in the first few weeks, they will stay. If they don't, they won't. Small churches may manage to do this informally, medium-sized and larger churches have to organize it through a 'Welcome Team' of lay members whose job it is to find people friends and integrate them into the small group or fellowship life of the church.

What proportion of the people who try your church once or twice actually join your community? What can you do to increase that proportion?

6. **Prevent people slipping away unnoticed.** Even committed Christians increasingly don't come to church every week. How do you know whether someone is not there this week because he is off with the caravan, again, or because she is lying in bed ill wondering whether the church people care? Most churches need to organize in order to keep a watchful pastoral eye on everyone, especially on those with less relational-glue to hold them into the church community. This can be done through a team of people who divide up the church membership between them in one way or another, or through developing a small-group network so that all have friends who care for them and who will notice if they start drifting away.

How easy is it to drift away unnoticed from your church? How can you care for people so well that they are truly at home and will never want to leave?

7. **Share the leadership.** If everything has to go through the vicar, your church will never grow larger than the vicar's capability. And there are fewer paid clergy to go round every year! But overburdened lay leaders can also burn out. Growing churches tend to succeed by sharing out the leadership not just in token ways but by giving real responsibility to a wide range of people.

What is your leadership structure and what does it do to

the leaders? How can genuine leadership be more widely spread?

8. **Improve the buildings.** Growing churches tend to improve the buildings for mission purposes, not just to make the existing people more comfortable.

What building work would make our premises more attractive to newcomers or enable us to start new ministries and congregations?

A lady trying a church for the first time was chatting over coffee after the service. 'We're a very friendly church here,' said the smiling regular. 'I don't want a friendly church,' retorted the newcomer, 'I want a church where I can make friends'.

3

Growing the Church through fresh expressions

(The Road to Growth Chapter 7)

This section comes from observing the new movement for planting fresh expressions of church given impetus by the report *Mission-shaped Church* (Church House Publishing, 2004). The trick is to be a 'both-and' church. It is foolish for traditionalists and radicals to fight each other – if the Church is to grow overall it needs to offer high quality tradition and innovation at the same time. That way it will reach more groups of people. We will fly best with two wings – traditional and fresh expressions – both supporting each other.

So this section is about re-imagining what it means to be church:

> *For where two or three are gathered in my name, I am there among them.*
>
> *Matthew 18.20*

Here are some examples of fresh expressions of church that seem to be making a significant contribution to overall growth today:

1. **Multiple congregations.** A church with one main Sunday morning service instead has two, one more traditional and one more contemporary.

2. **Weekday congregations.** Churches are trying many different service times and styles in attempts to match the contemporary 24/7 culture. Examples include teatime family

services; midweek evening worship events for people working or away on Sundays; care home services; children's groups and worship after school instead of 'Sunday school'; lunch-club worship; lunch-break worship for town centre workers, and so on.

3. **Church plants.** The classic planting of a daughter church roughly in the image of the mother church but more informal in a more informal setting elsewhere in the parish or area is still a fruitful source of church growth.

4. **Café church.** Instead of sitting in rows on pews, the people sit round tables with food and drink. The atmosphere is more informal and the service more interactive. Small-group discussion becomes a natural part of the event.

5. **Network churches.** Some people relate better to their own networks built up from their contacts at work, through leisure pursuits and stage of life affiliation than they do to geographic communities and churches. My own diocese has a policy of employing a network-church planter for young adults in every major population centre.

6. **Schools–linked congregations.** Schools are making good premises for new congregations, for example, at going home time or at 4.30 p.m. on a Saturday. The school is where the people gather naturally already and they are already familiar with it. The premises are often well suited to the needs of congregations, and headteachers are often sympathetic.

7. **Turning events into church.** The traditional means by which church events such as a parent and toddler group or a lunch club or a youth club are used for mission is to see them as contact points and halfway houses to attract people to the real church that happens on Sunday mornings in the proper building. A different and sometimes more fruitful approach is to work towards the event becoming church for the people who already attend it.

8. **Cell church.** In the pure form of 'cell church' the small cell is the church and the first call on members' time commitment

– the Sunday celebration being the second. This can suit the pattern of postmodern lives and also attitudes – many younger adults find small groups easier to cope with than traditional congregations in pews.

9. **Youth congregations.** Churches that expect their teenagers to join in with the OAPs' worship tend to lose them just as fast as they would lose the OAPs if they were made to join in youth worship. Specialist youth worship events are proving successful in many places in a variety of styles. It is often important for churches to join together so that one event is on the programme of several churches and a large enough group of young people is gathered together.

What are attitudes like in your church? How can you help everyone to honour and support both traditional ways and new ways of doing church?

Has your church started any new events recently that could be termed 'fresh expressions'? Review how they are going.

Given the types of people who live in your area, or are associated with your church, what sort of fresh expression might work well where you are?

Fifty people came to the church's Wednesday lunch club, but hardly any of them came to the service on a Sunday. So the vicar moved the midweek communion service to 45 minutes before the start of the lunch club and invited the members to come early if they wished to. To his surprise, most of them did and suddenly the midweek congregation was as big as the Sunday one. Rather than expecting those who attended the event to start coming to church, the event had become church for those who attended it.

4

Growing the Church through diocesan policy and shared values

(The Road to Growth Chapter 8)

This section comes from researching the reasons for the growth of churches in the Diocese of London and the 'New Wine' network.

It is about how churches that used to be shaky become solid rocks:

> *You are Peter, and on this rock I will build my church.*
> *Matthew 16.18*

1. **Mission action plans.** From the early 1990s every parish in the Diocese of London has been asked to produce its own mission action plan (MAP). For some parishes all three concepts in a MAP were novelties. Advisers were appointed to help parishes implement their MAPs as well as simply devise them.

   Does your church have well thought-out mission plans? If so, do they need updating or implementing? If not, what should your church's MAP look like?

2. **Clergy as leaders in mission.** London diocese also started looking for new types of clergy, or at least at having new job descriptions for vacant posts. No longer was the aim simply to find a servant of a particular tradition or a pastor for a particular flock but rather it became to find someone who could lead the church into mission and growth.

   What sort of job description does your vicar or minister

have? Are too many expectations placed upon him or her? Is there even a job description? What should be the core priority for your clergy?*

3. **Small can be beautiful.** As elsewhere, the fastest growing churches in London have been the smaller ones. It is much easier to double a congregation of 20 than one of 200. Such churches grow on relationships, community, and the personal ministry of clergy and leaders.

   If your church is small, how can you harness the advantages of your size in order to grow bigger?

4. **Social enterprise.** Churches that engage in social enterprise in areas of deprivation can experience church growth as a spin-off benefit, although this does not work as the main motive.

   Is your church trying to grow as a private club or as a force for good in the community?

5. **Transplanting groups.** Some of the growth has come about when a group has left a large church at the request of the bishop or vicar and joined a small, struggling one with the aim of being a core group for new growth.

   Is there any scope for transplanting in your area?

6. **Growing younger.** Both in London and in New Wine churches it is the younger congregations – and those with younger clergy – that are growing best.

   How can your church become more in tune with people aged under 35 and grow through attracting them?

7. **Worship as encounter.** A key New Wine value is that worship should be passionate and joyful, full of expectation of encounter with the living God. Growing churches tend to include testimonies and interviews regularly in their church services. Emphasis is on the reality of faith, on personal experience.

   How can your church increase the reality of its encounter with God? How can church services become unique and engaging experiences rather than boring routine?

8. **Orthodox in theology, radical in form.** Churches of all theologies and traditions are able to grow today. Many growth-friendly attributes are available to all churches. However, growing churches are clearly more likely to be conservative in theology and radical in form. The faith is best preserved by the renewal of the church, not by its fossilization.

What should your church be radical about and what should it be conservative about?

The previous vicar had left to become a Roman Catholic, and most of the congregation joined him. The remaining few were set in their ways. The new vicar networked around the local community and transformed the worship style – from heavy, formal and mysterious to friendly, informal and accessible, though still recognizably catholic. It was the same faith but a different culture. Young families began to turn up. Before long, numbers had risen from ten to a hundred.

5

Growing the Church through deploying the clergy

(The Road to Growth Chapters 10 and 11)

This section comes from researching the links between features of the clergy and the growth of the Church. All stories of major church growth seem to start with the appointment of a new incumbent. Numerical research suggests that the ageing of the clergy is probably our most important church-growth handicap and that the lengthening of vacancies is the major single cause of church decline today.

So this section is about the key role of the clergy:

> *Let no one despise your youth, but set the believers an example in speech and conduct, in love, in faith, in purity ... give attention to the public reading of scripture, to exhorting, to teaching.*
>
> *1 Timothy 4.12,13*

1. **Combat the problems of teams.** Attendance trends in team rector and team vicar parishes are significantly worse than in single-vicar parishes. Clergy and others have more time taken up with internal meetings and relationships, and so have less time and focus for external mission. And there is much more scope for conflict. We need simple arrangements that encourage an outward-looking focus. The same applies to Local Educational Partnerships (LEPs) and other similar arrangements.

   If you are in a team situation, do you have too many layers

*of meetings and governance? Who is in charge of the team
vicar's church – the team rector, the team vicar, the PCC or
the DCC?*

2. **Look for young clergy.** Years ago we started telling potential
   young clergy to 'go away, get a proper job in the real world
   for a few years and come back when you are mature'. Yet
   younger clergy are more likely to attract younger
   congregations and growing congregations. Now we are very
   anxious to find as many young clergy as possible.

   *How often does your church produce ordinands? How can
   you best encourage people in their late teens and twenties
   to think about ordination or other church leadership
   roles?*

3. **Care for older clergy.** Older clergy, such as myself, have much
   to offer, including the wisdom of experience. But many are
   tired and some are beginning to slip out of touch with
   younger generations. Some get bored or demotivated after
   many years in essentially the same job. Most can be helped
   by a break from relentless parish duties, the stimulus of
   younger colleagues, and fresh job descriptions and
   challenges.

   *What contribution can your church make to the well-
   being of your clergy, to help keep them fresh and
   effective?*

4. **Find people for jobs not jobs for people.** The cause of church
   growth and development is probably not best served by
   patronage centred on the need of a particular clergy person
   for a new job. It is better to centre on the job description and
   person specification needed to be a successful leader in
   mission and then to go looking for a suitable candidate.

   *As and when you look for a new minister, what sort of
   person and job specification would best help your church
   to grow?*

5. **Make appointments quickly.** On average, churches with
   incumbents are growing numerically. The Church of

England's usual Sunday attendance, however, has still gone down slightly in the early twenty-first century because of large losses in churches with vacancies of over six months. Some dioceses even have policies for long vacancies – say nine or fifteen months. No other organization allows such a long gap between local managers or leaders.

Has your church ever suffered from a long vacancy? What can you do to prepare for your next vacancy? Can you persuade your diocese to keep it short?

The vicar was reaching 60 and his health was no longer so good. There were fewer children around on a Sunday and things were beginning to drift downwards. But the diocese gave him a young curate, a key church member retired and offered his time to the church, and a combination of the diocesan growth fund and generosity from church members paid for a children's worker. Suddenly there was a new staff team, including two people in their twenties. There was new energy, numbers went up quite sharply, especially at the younger end, and the vicar himself was re-energized – perhaps he had saved the best till last after all!

6

Growing the Church through lay leadership and training

(*The Road to Growth* Chapter 11)

This section comes from research into the impact on parish life of diocesan leadership training schemes and other strategies for equipping the Church for life with fewer paid clergy.

It is about activating the whole body of Christ for the ministry of the Church:

> *Now you are the body of Christ and individually members of it.*
>
> 1 *Corinthians 12.27*

1. **Beware of filling the gaps.** Numbers of stipendiary clergy continue to go down in many dioceses, either through financial constraints or through shrinking numbers of clergy available. Some dioceses have put a lot of effort into schemes to train a small group of lay members, often including an OLM, to conduct ministry that was formerly the preserve of the paid clergy. Churches that have had a 'lay ministry team' train on such a course have often experienced shrinkage as a result. Some of their key people have been taken from their key jobs and trained for three years to do something else. The focus of church life became inward – training people to do the jobs to keep the show going – rather than outward. Sometimes the 'minister' is simply replaced by the 'ministry team' and the rest of the church is still the passive recipient of its ministry. Yet we all agree that

help and training for an every-member ministry church must be a good thing!

So what is the best way to offer help and training to lay leaders for the sorts of ministry that will grow your church? Do you want a small 'lay ministry team' or 'every member ministry'?

2. **Grow people-shaped churches, not church-shaped people.** People today are less happy than older generations were to do jobs in the church that don't quite suit them. Rather than stuff round pegs into square holes, it is often better to allow the energy and gifting of individuals to determine their contribution to the life of the church.

   Where are our energy and gifting directed and are we able to exercise the ministry to which we feel God has equipped and called us?

3. **Become a missionary community.** Church growth in a post-Christian or a non-Christian culture comes from having a missionary mindset. For the sake of people who would be attracted by a loving, joyful church community, it is everyone's responsibility to contribute to that attractive community. Today people initially tend to be more interested in whether Christianity works than in whether it is true, so it is every member's responsibility to be ready to tell his or her own story of how being a Christian works in practice.

   How well can the members of our church tell their God-stories? Do we even tell them to each other in order to encourage one another or to practise the telling? How can we best equip ourselves to witness to our faith?

4. **Learn to network.** There are many thousands of churches around the country and many of them have found superb ways of growing and flourishing. Individual churches do not need to keep reinventing the wheel. One of the keys to the growth of New Wine churches is that they are plugged in to a

helpful network. Find and use networks or ask your diocese to facilitate them. Learn good practice from each other.

How often does your church learn something new from another church and how often do you pass on the things you learn? In what area of church life do you most need help today and where can you get it from?

5. **Pay lay people.** Every-member ministry may be a great aim but how feasible is it in an age where jobs and general living have become more demanding and stressful? Many good Christians can see church only as a resource to keep them going. We have less leisure but we have more money. Realistic giving levels should mean that many individual churches and all groupings of small churches have the power to pay lay people for specialist ministries. The number of youth ministers, children's workers, administrators, pastoral care managers, and so on, seems to be growing. Churches that have put together a talented, committed paid leadership team with a mix of young and old, male and female, lay and ordained, tend to be growing.

From what sorts of post and people could your church most benefit? How could the vision for this be realized in practice? Where would the money come from?

The warden and other leaders of a village church wanted to share their faith but felt tongue-tied. They met together as a home group over a period of months in order to tell each other their Christian stories. By learning to tell each other their experiences of God in the safety of the group they became more able to witness to others about the reality of God in their lives.

7

Growing the Church through sound finances

(The Road to Growth Chapters 12–17)

This section comes from observing share systems and other financial structures in many parishes and dioceses. Jesus talked about money an awful lot – how we deal with our money is at the heart of our spirituality.

Financial structures can either empower or undermine the growth of churches, but mostly this section is about our financial attitudes and the way they release or withhold the resources needed to enable churches to grow:

> *Do not store up for yourselves treasures on earth ...*
> *but ... treasures in heaven ... For where your treasure*
> *is, there your heart will be also.*
>
> *Matthew 6.19–21*

1. **Know your parish share system.** Every diocese has its own system of allocating the financial call upon the parishes to pay the cost of the clergy and their support. All systems have their faults and all are controversial! However, some hinder growth more than others. For example a 'poll tax' system of allocating share according to last year's average attendance can drive churches into financial crisis when they start to grow because the new people don't give at the rate of the others and because growth can often be sustained only by great internal expenditure on assistant staff.

Do you understand your own share system? Do you know

how your parish share is spent by your diocese? What impact does it have on the growth of your church?

2. **Be advocates of Christian giving rather than church taxation.** Parish share systems that feel like centrally planned taxation do not normally bring out enthusiasm and Christian virtue in parishes. Churches may flourish better given freedom and responsibility for self-funding and for giving to churches that cannot self-fund. Arguments about share systems are complex and not for everyone. They are rehearsed at length in *The Road to Growth.*

   What sort of share arrangement would best support the growth of your church? And what sort would best support the growth of churches that are different from you? What changes would you advocate to the way your diocese organizes things?

3. **Contribute your expertise to your diocese.** Most dioceses employ a substantial number of non-parish staff – in finance departments, as parish advisers, chaplains, and so on. Some parishes resent this expenditure, believing their share gets lost down a diocesan black hole. Diocesan central costs certainly need controlling to be in proportion to the parish staff they are supposed to be supporting.

   For the good and growth of every parish, does your church have people with expertise to serve diocesan synods and committees in order to promote the efficiency of the diocese in the cause of the kingdom of heaven?

4. **Find a development budget.** Almost all diocesan and church expenditure seems to be spent on keeping going as much as possible from the past. Organizations without a development budget tend not to be long for this world. The Church Commissioners now channel a 'mission initiatives' funding stream to dioceses. My own diocese, for example, now has a 'growth fund', mainly funded by the Church Commissioners, to which churches can apply for grants for church growth initiatives. The diocese is now not only asking

churches to develop and grow but also offering them financial resources to empower their growth. Individual churches should also have a development budget that is discretionary spending for the year ahead, not committed in advance to the maintaining of one function or another.

Does your diocese have a development fund for making grants? Can you encourage it to set one up? How can your church set aside significant money to develop its own life and ministry? Can you give money away to other churches, who could use it for their evangelism and growth?

5. **Teach Christian giving.** Churches where the people give generously back to God in response to his generosity to them tend not to be held back by financial constraints. Churches relying on fund-raising will almost always be limited in what they can achieve. Churches with a shared vision of the way forward will normally find that the people fund the vision. Churches without unity or without vision will normally struggle.

How in your church can you best change your heart attitudes to unlock your joyful giving? How can you make stewardship initiatives more effective? What example should you be giving to others?

In the Diocese of Down and Dromore in Northern Ireland, the churches own their own vicarages and pay their own clergy. There are very few diocesan staff and no parish share is required. The cost base is lower and neither the churches nor the diocese seem to have difficult financial problems. They think they have found a better arrangement for their finances and organization than English dioceses, but are they right?

8

Growing the Church through spiritual renewal

(The Road to Growth Chapter 18)

This section comes not so much from numerical research as from a close observation of church life across the country over the last 40 years. Healthy growth never comes from changes or policies that are purely organizational or human. These things work only on the back of a healthy and deepening spirituality. Commitment matters more than structures. What are the important touchstones today?

So this section is about taking and raising the spiritual temperature of the Church:

> *Because you are lukewarm, and neither cold nor hot, I am about to spit you out of my mouth.*
>
> *Revelation 3.16*

1. **Recognize that God is at work.** The Church of England is changing fast. There are several widespread movements of renewal in the churches today – the evangelism courses, the rise of small groups and lay ministry, the fresh expressions, the church planting, the mass conferences, gatherings and networks such as Spring Harvest and New Wine, and the new retreat, monastic and pilgrimage movements such as Walsingham, Cursillo and 'Order of Mission'. The Spirit is on the move. A century of decline appears to be halting, perhaps just for the moment, perhaps as a prelude to an era of growth.

Where do you see God's hand at work in the renewal of your own church and of church life locally in your area? What is there to make you optimistic and excited about the future?

2. **Rekindle the passion.** Lukewarm Christians lack the energy and attractiveness to form growing churches. Churches grow when the people are passionate about their faith and the business of sharing it. You do not have to be demonstrative to be passionate. In fact, people can't expect to retain their spiritual passion simply through repeating an extrovert form of worship Sunday by Sunday. It is hard for shallow churches to stay on the boil. Renewal of spiritual passion can come in many ways, but it does not come without new challenge and new depth leading to new maturity.

How passionate are the people of your church? What is the best way of raising the spiritual temperature?

3. **Encourage experience.** Church services should be vehicles for religious experience. Services structured to maximize the chances of people having an encounter with God tend to attract. Churches in which members share their experiences of God with each other grow in confidence and expectation.

How do people experience God through your church? How can you provide good opportunities for encounters to take place?

4. **Pray together.** Compared with 40 years ago, there has been a great advance in prayer – now the people of our churches lead the Sunday intercessions and pray together in small groups. Churches that pray together grow together. There is no point in prayer-less church growth strategies. But prayer needs to be serious and sacrificial.

How effective is the corporate prayer life of your church? How can you best pray together for the extension of Christ's kingdom through the growth of his Church?

5. **Centre on the Bible.** Growing churches tend to take the Bible

increasingly seriously. There are worries that some churches sit more lightly to the Bible than they used to: sermons are shorter; experience matters more than truth or teaching; people don't bring Bibles to church anymore; children don't know or memorize it the way they used to. Yet there are new ways of getting in to the Bible these days as well, for example through the use of the Internet or of data projectors. And the Bible brings experience of God as well as knowledge of him.

What imaginative new ways can you think of for allowing the Bible to have an impact on the life of your church? How can you help new Christians get excited about reading it?

6. **Love one another.** This was Jesus' great command to his Church. If anything, a loving church is an even bigger magnet in this day and age when so many people have lost their sense of local community and belonging and so many families have broken apart in divorce and separation. Church communities that are secure places of acceptance and love are increasingly attractive.

   How well do the people of your church love one another, especially the people on the fringe or who don't quite fit in? How can you renew your commitment to each other?

7. **Listen to what the Spirit says to the churches.** If your church wants to grow it is important to listen to the guidance of God, to the voice of his Spirit telling you how to go about it. You may wish to set aside quiet days, half nights of prayer and other special events for this. And you will certainly want to pray for God's guidance in the regular round of church services, small groups and church council meetings.

   Can you share with each other what you think the Holy Spirit is saying to your church about your future direction and growth?

We visited a church on holiday. It was a good service with an excellent sermon. But the thing we remember some weeks later was the lady who told us the story of what God had done in her life that week – a dramatic story about learning to forgive and be reconciled.

Using this material for small groups

This guidebook is designed for flexible use by different types of church groups, for example by church councils. However, the following material will enable it to be used in small groups as a tool for renewing church life and strategy over a period of weeks. The material here is in cell group style but it is easily adaptable for use by other study or home groups. Typically, a cell group will use the fourfold structure of 'Welcome–Worship–Word–Witness'.

Each of the eight sections easily forms the 'Witness' material for a cell group meeting for each at heart is about how your church can witness more effectively. This would form the main event of the meeting and the 'Welcome', 'Worship' and 'Word' sections would be truncated for the duration of the course while still keeping to cell principles.

Reporting back from the small group to the centre would be especially important as the eight-week course is geared at finding new impetus and strategy for the growth and development of the whole church. You will need to devise your own way of doing this. Below are the outlines for eight group meetings.

Suggested timings if following the cell format are:

Welcome (10 minutes): ice-breaker.

Worship (10–15 minutes): prayer and/or singing either after the Welcome or at the end of the meeting.

Word (10–15 minutes): Bible passage discussion before the Witness section.

Witness (1 hour): Using the material from the appropriate section of this book.

Group members should each have a copy of the book and should read and think about the appropriate section before the meeting.

Week 1

Welcome: What day and time would you pick for your church service and your cell group if it were up to you? Give your reasons!

Worship: Pray for any teenagers in your church, for anyone doing an Alpha or similar course at the moment, and for God to bring in any missing or under-represented age group to your church.

Word: Read 1 Corinthians 3.5–9. Discuss: If the church is God's field or garden and it is God who makes it grow, what is the job of church leaders and members?

Witness: Section 1 of this book.

Week 2

Welcome: Share your stories of how you joined your church. Was it easy or hard to break in? How quickly did you start to make friends?

Worship: Thank and praise God for any recent changes for the better in the life of your church and for changes in your own life in which God has had a hand.

Word: Read Philippians 3.12–16. Discuss: What is a mature Christian attitude to change?

Witness: Section 2 of this book.

Week 3

Welcome: Swap stories of attending church services or events or fresh expressions of church that were different from the ordinary. Think of the best or the worst one you have ever been to.

Worship: Praise God that he is inclusive – his love and his offer of forgiveness and resurrection life are for every type and individual. Pray for unity within diversity in the Church.

Word: Read Matthew 18.19, 20. Discuss: What does it mean to be church? How far can you go in classifying a meeting or event as 'being church'?

Witness: Section 3 of this book.

Week 4

Welcome: Think of an occasion in which you felt you encountered God in a church service or event or a cell group. Some may be too personal and intimate to share, but no doubt some of you will have an entertaining or moving story to tell.

Worship: Praise God for his dynamism through time and history, that our world is moving through its stages to the climax when Jesus will return. Thank him for his plans for your church's future mission.

Word: Read Matthew 16.13–18. Discuss: Jesus promises to build his church on a human rock. But not every individual church grows and survives. What does Jesus' promise mean for our own church today?

Witness: Section 4 of this book.

Week 5

Welcome: Who is the most eccentric or amusing or outstanding vicar you have known?

Worship: Thank God for calling people to ordination and pray for the next generation of clergy to be found and trained.

Word: Read 1 Timothy 4.11–16. Discuss: Suppose you have a new vicar and he or she is only 27 years old. What special problems and opportunities might result from this?

Witness: Section 5 of this book.

Week 6

Welcome: What jobs have you had in a church or elsewhere to which you were really unsuited?

Worship: Praise God for the gifts, talents, ministries and spiritual energy of the other members of the group.

Word: Read 1 Corinthians 12.27–31. Discuss: God has given gifts to us all. Should we just allow our gifts and inclinations to decide what we do in the church and in life generally or should we also look at the needs and see how we can meet them, even if we move outside our comfort zone?

Witness: Section 6 of this book.

Week 7

Welcome: Can you remember buying something that was a complete waste of money?

Worship: Praise God for the wealth of the world and for the part of that wealth over which he has allowed you to have some control.

Word: Read Matthew 6.19–21. What heart attitude to money will enable a church to have all the resources it needs to perform its God-given mission?

Witness: Section 7 of this book.

Week 8

Welcome: Have you ever come across any unusual 'new age' type spirituality?

Worship: Thank God that he is changing you as part of his plan to grow Christians fit to share heaven with him. Ask him to hurry up a little.

Word: Read Revelation 3.14–22. How can we tell what the Spirit is saying to our church, especially if it is something not very comfortable?

Witness: Section 8 of this book.

Further reading from Church House Publishing

Christian Roots, Contemporary Spirituality
Lynda Barley
£6.99   0 7151 4102 3   A5   72 pages

Lynda Barley – Head of Research and Statistics for the Church of England – looks at recent social trends and attitudes towards church, God and belief. Her analysis shows that the Christian faith still has a place at the heart of the nation. Combining analysis with real life stories, she encourages the Church to take advantage of this residual inherited faith in order to engage with the spiritual needs of those outside the Church.

Churchgoing Today
Lynda Barley
£6.99   0 7151 4103 1   A5   72 pages

Weekly Sunday attendance may be in decline, but churches that adapt to the needs of the community are experiencing growth. There are further signs of hope in the thousands of fresh expressions of church springing up throughout the UK. Combining analysis with real-life stories, she encourages the Church to take seriously the need to adapt and enlarge its vision in order to stem the decline in church attendance.

Mission–shaped Spirituality
The transforming power of mission
Sue Hope
£7.99   0 7151 4080 9   A5   144 pages

If your shelves are overloaded with books on how to *do* mission, create some space to engage with this book. No to-do lists. No win-win strategies. Instead this discerning book reflects on the inner resources and attitude of mind required to engage in mission in a post-modern, pluralist society. This gently provocative book will help us to listen to the Holy Spirit and the cultures in which we find ourselves.

Evangelism in a Spiritual Age
Communicating faith in a changing culture
Steven Croft, Rob Frost, Mark Ireland, Anne Richards,
Yvonne Richmond, Nick Spencer
£11.99   0 7151 4054 X   234 × 156mm   176 pages

This ground-breaking book analyses how to understand the spirituality of people who don't go to church and points to ways of communicating the gospel more effectively to them. It unpacks the big questions people are asking; how people view Christians and the Church; looks at general trends in spirituality and creative evangelism and addresses the key importance of listening and community. This book offers challenging, yet accessible responses showing how the Church might address the issue of evangelism in the twenty-first century.

The Healthy Churches' Handbook
A process for revitalizing your church
Robert Warren
£10.95   0 7151 4017 5   234 × 156mm   176 pages

Developed out of the *Growing Healthy Churches* material, this practical guide helps churches identify their strengths and weaknesses and discover what action to take in order to develop the health of their church. The focus is on the *quality* of the Church's life rather than just the numbers attending. The goal is not to find easy solutions, but rather to encounter the reality of God's presence in and through the life of each church.